Tic-Tac-Toe Math

for Grades 3 and 4

DAVE CLARK

Dale Seymour Publications®
Orangeburg, New York

Managing Editor: Catherine Anderson
Production Manager: Janet Yearian
Project Editor: Joan Gideon
Production Coordinator: Joe Conte
Art: Rachel Gage
Cover Design: Don Taka

Published by Dale Seymour Publications®, an imprint of
Addison Wesley Longman, Inc.

Dale Seymour Publications
125 Greenbush Road South
Orangeburg, New York 10962
Customer Service: 800-872-1100

Order Number DS21856
ISBN 1-57232-977-7

3 4 5 6 7 8 9 10-VG-01

This product is printed
on recycled paper

Introduction

A Note to Parents and Teachers

This book of engaging puzzles provides practice of mathematics concepts and skills as well as a variety of problem-solving techniques. The Skills Planner (pages v and vi) shows what games to use for practicing particular skills. The game rules are simple but flexible – they may be modified to suit the needs of individual children.

These games can be played individually, in pairs, in small groups, or as a whole-class activity. Teachers may use *Tic-Tac-Toe* Math either as a student workbook or a set of blackline masters, while most parents will use it as a puzzle or game book for their children.

The rules for several *Tic-Tac-Toe Math* variations are on the next page. Although they have been written so that most children will be able to read and follow them, teachers or parents should go through the rules with the children when first introducing the games.

Classroom Hint: Laminate the pages. Have children use scrap paper to find the answers and different kinds of markers or counters to mark their squares.

Tic-Tac-Toe Math Game Rules

These rules will help you start playing *Tic-Tac-Toe Math* games. After you try these rules, you may think of other ways to play these games.

Tic-Tac-Toe Math for One Player

- Solve all the problems. Then check your answers.
- A tic-tac-toe is three correct answers in a row.
  Scoring: 1 point for each correct answer.
  1 point for each tic-tac-toe.
  A perfect score is 17 points. See how close you can come to this score.

Two Tic-Tac-Toe Math Games for Two Players

- For both games, take turns choosing a square as in regular tic-tac-toe. Before you mark the square (or put a counter or marker on it), write the answer to the question in the box (or on another piece of paper).
- Game 1: When one player gets three in a row, check the answers. If an answer is incorrect, change the mark (or marker) on that square to that of the other player. Play until one player wins with three correct answers in a row.
- Game 2: Play as above, but fill in the entire board before checking the answers. If an answer is incorrect, change that mark (or marker) to that of the other player. The winner is the player who has more tic-tac-toes.

Two Tic-Tac-Toe Math Games for Any Number of Players

- Game 1: Give a copy of the game to each player. Each player solves as many problems as possible. Score as a one-player game and compare scores.
- Game 2: Give copies of several games to each player. Each player finishes as many problems as possible in a given time (for example, 10 minutes). Some players may complete more than one game. Score as a one-player game and compare scores.

Skills Planner

Skill	Game Number
Addition	1, 2, 4, 6, 7, 8, 9, 13, 14, 15, 17, 20, 22, 24, 27, 29, 30, 31, 32, 33, 40, 42, 43, 44, 45, 46, 50, 54, 60, 64, 65, 66, 71
Addition facts	1, 2, 3, 4, 5, 6, 7, 8, 9, 12, 13, 14, 20, 21, 22, 25, 26, 28, 29, 31, 32, 42, 45, 48, 63
Algebra	30, 44, 47, 53
Alphabet math	16, 21, 42, 68, 74
Area	49, 53, 56, 57, 60, 74
Average	63, 65, 69, 71, 78
Calendar	1, 2, 5, 6, 13, 16, 20, 27, 36, 40, 43, 48, 56, 68, 69, 73, 77
Circles, radius and diameter	75
Critical Thinking	1, 3, 5, 27, 30, 41, 47, 49, 53, 56, 67, 71, 78
Decimals	29, 30, 32, 38, 39, 42, 54, 57, 58, 63, 64, 69, 73, 76, 77, 78, 80
Division facts	31, 32, 36, 50, 58, 61, 67, 71
Division	33, 34, 35, 37, 41, 49, 51, 52, 54, 55, 56, 63, 66, 68
Fact families	43, 46, 49, 51, 52, 55, 57
Factors	75, 76
Fractions	39, 69, 72, 73, 74, 78, 79, 80
Functions	44, 48, 69, 73, 75, 76, 77
Geometry	47, 64
Identifying missing digits	14, 19, 67, 70, 78
Inverse operations	1, 11, 12, 16, 17, 18, 19, 27, 37, 50, 51, 57, 58, 61, 63, 64, 67, 71, 74
Math vocabulary	2, 8, 9, 10, 14, 17, 28, 29, 32, 33, 40, 41, 42, 43, 44, 47, 48, 49, 54, 55, 57, 58, 59, 61, 65, 67, 69, 70, 71, 72, 73, 75, 76, 77, 78
Measurement conversions	3, 6, 8, 9, 13, 15, 18, 20, 21, 22, 29, 34, 36, 38, 39, 40, 46, 48, 52, 55, 63, 64, 69, 71, 73, 74, 77, 80
Money	1, 2, 3, 4, 5, 6, 9, 10, 11, 12, 14, 15, 16, 18, 19, 20, 21, 22, 23, 24, 26, 27, 29, 30, 31, 32, 33, 35, 37, 38, 40, 41, 42, 44, 46, 50, 52, 55, 56, 58, 60, 61, 62, 63, 65, 66, 67, 71, 76, 78
Multiples	44, 48, 49, 72, 73, 76

Skills Planner

Skill	Game Number
Multiplication facts	1, 3, 4, 14, 18, 23, 24, 25, 26, 27, 28, 29, 30, 31, 32, 33, 34, 35, 36, 37, 42, 47, 51, 54, 58, 63, 71, 71, 75, 77, 78
Multiplication	5, 27, 28, 29, 30, 33, 36, 38, 42, 47, 48, 49, 50, 52, 54, 55, 56, 58, 59, 61, 62, 64, 65, 66, 68, 69, 70, 73, 78
Number names	8, 22, 23, 24, 26, 37, 38, 39, 41, 46, 48, 51, 57, 59, 60, 61, 62, 64, 66, 67, 73, 74, 78, 79
Odd or even numbers	19, 26, 30, 40, 51, 65, 77, 80
One-half	25, 37, 39, 45, 57, 62, 69, 71
Ordering decimal numbers	79, 80
Perimeter	3, 6, 7, 10, 14, 27, 41, 42, 48, 53, 56, 57, 60, 74, 75
Place value	2, 11, 13, 31, 35, 37, 41, 43, 45, 47, 50, 53, 60, 69, 70, 72, 73, 75, 77
Problem solving: drawing pictures	79
Problem solving: guess and check	1, 4, 7, 11, 12, 18, 21, 22, 23, 26, 27, 28, 30, 31, 34, 36, 43, 46, 50, 52, 53, 56, 57, 58, 60, 61, 66, 71, 75, 76, 77, 80
Problem solving: look for a pattern	5, 37, 41, 65, 70
Problem solving: make a chart	75
Problem solving: organized lists	24, 32, 43, 44, 63, 74, 77
Problem solving: work backwards	54
Probability	70, 78
Proportion	74
Roman numerals	12, 62, 68, 71
Rounding/ estimation	20, 35, 44, 46, 53 58, 60, 70, 74, 76, 80
Story problems	1, 3, 4, 5, 6, 7, 8, 9, 12, 15, 16, 17, 19, 20, 21, 23, 24, 25, 26, 29, 30, 32, 33, 34, 35, 36, 37, 38, 39, 40, 43, 45, 47, 48, 50, 51, 53, 54, 55, 58, 59, 61, 64, 67, 68, 80
Subtraction facts	1, 2, 3, 4, 5, 6, 7, 8, 9, 12, 13, 18, 20, 21, 22, 25, 26, 31, 47, 71
Subtraction	4, 6, 7, 8, 12, 13, 15, 16, 17, 19, 20, 21, 23, 28, 29, 30, 31, 32, 38, 41, 44, 45, 52, 54, 55, 57, 58, 59, 62, 65, 68
Temperature	45, 56
Time	14, 16, 18, 20, 23, 24, 30, 31, 40, 46

Name ______________________________

Game 1

$8 + 3 =$ $8 - 3 =$	Cross out the number that does not belong. 2 10 16 7 8 Explain your answer.	$11 - \square = 3$ $11 - \square = 8$
How many days are in February if it is not a leap year?	Find 2 numbers whose sum is 17 and whose difference is 1.	How many paws do 4 cats and 9 dogs have all together?
At a store, I spent the following amounts: \$4.26, \$7.49, and \$6.89. How much did I spend in all?	I saved 10 cents each day in June. How much did I have at the end of the month?	$3 + 3 + 3 =$ $3 \times 3 =$

Name ______________________________

Game 2

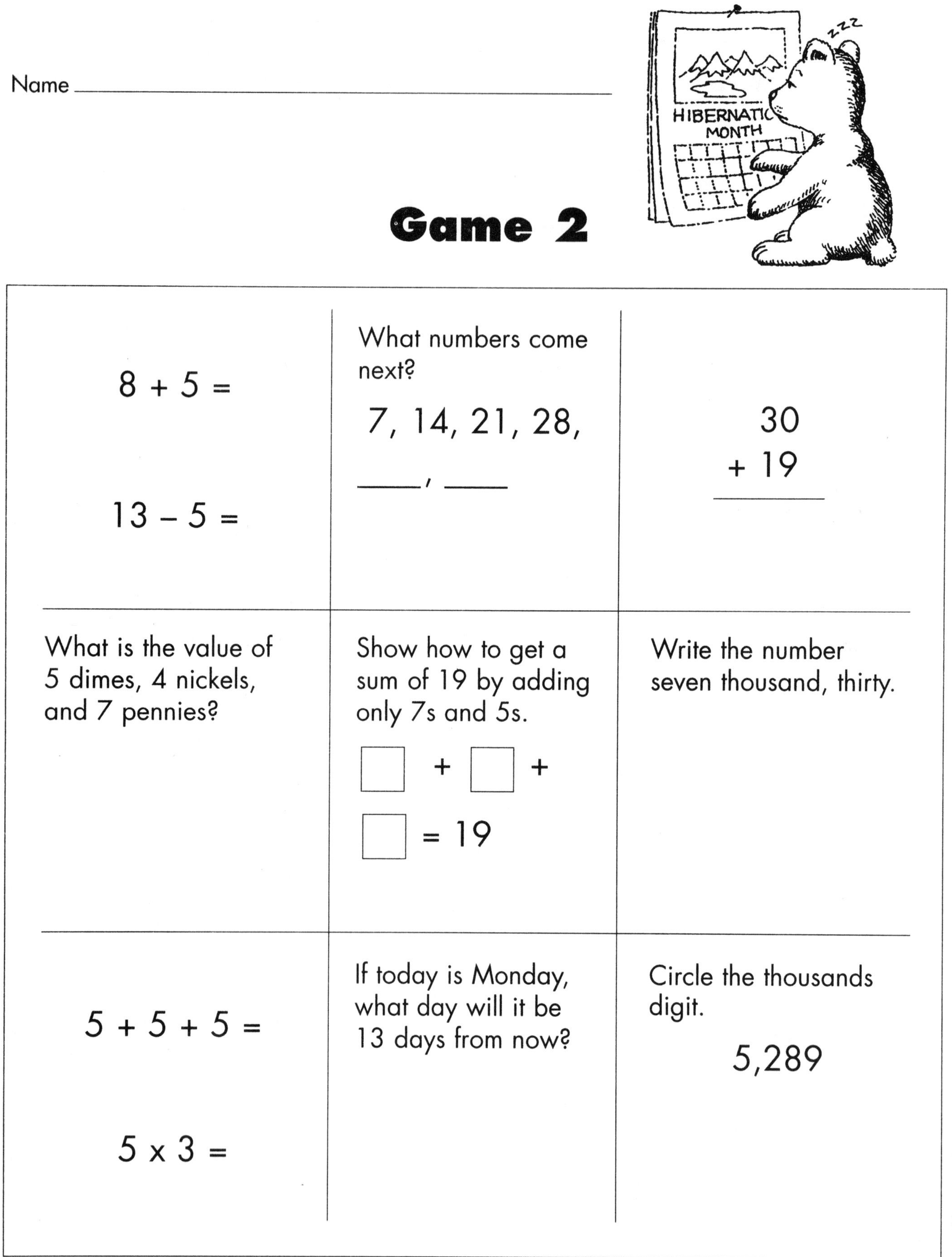

8 + 5 = 13 – 5 =	What numbers come next? 7, 14, 21, 28, ____, ____	30 + 19 ____
What is the value of 5 dimes, 4 nickels, and 7 pennies?	Show how to get a sum of 19 by adding only 7s and 5s. ☐ + ☐ + ☐ = 19	Write the number seven thousand, thirty.
5 + 5 + 5 = 5 x 3 =	If today is Monday, what day will it be 13 days from now?	Circle the thousands digit. 5,289

Name ______________________________

Game 3

8 + 6 = 14 – 6 =	Cross out the number that does not belong. 3 6 7 9 12 Explain your answer.	How many feet are in 1 yard?
How many $10 bills equal $1,000?	Find the perimeter. 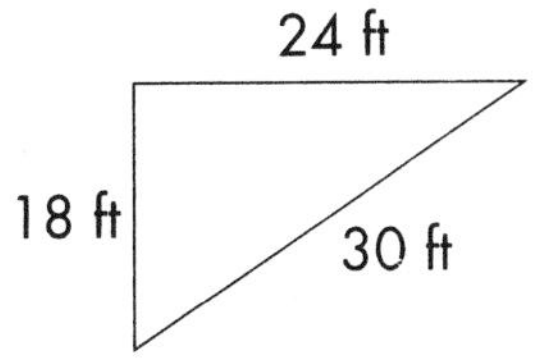	How many legs do 10 horses and 5 cows have all together?
$\begin{array}{r} 35 \\ +\ 25 \\ \hline \end{array}$	I save $3.00 each month for a year. How much did I save for the whole year?	2 + 2 + 2 = 2 x 3 =

Name ______________________________

Game 4

$7 + 8 =$ $15 - 8 =$	I had 15 pennies, but I lost 7 of them. How many pennies do I have now?	$\begin{array}{r} 302 \\ +\ 708 \\ \hline \end{array}$
I had 17 trading cards. I gave my friend 9 of my cards, and he gave me 5 of his cards. How many cards do I have now?	What numbers come next? 0, 3, 6, 9, 12, ____ , ____	I have 7 pencils. You have 8 pencils. How many pencils do we have together?
$\begin{array}{r} 656 \\ -\ 445 \\ \hline \end{array}$	I am thinking of a number. When you add 25 to my number, you get 30. What do you get when you subtract 2 from my number?	$10 + 10 + 10 =$ $10 \times 3 =$

Name ______________________________

Game 5

$7 + 7 =$

$14 - 7 =$

Cross out the number that does not belong.

5 9 15 10 20

Explain your answer.

Write a multiplication problem that describes this drawing.

4

4

☐ x ☐ = ☐

How many days are in March?

What number comes next?

2, 4, 8, 16, ___

How many paws do 15 lions and 8 tigers have all together?

$8 + 8 =$

$16 - 8 =$

I save $1.25 each week. How much will I save in 4 weeks?

If this had 3 more rows, what would be the last number?

1	2	3	4	5
6	7	8	9	10
11	12	13	14	15
16	17	18	19	20
21	22	23	24	25

Name ______________________________

Game 6

<table>
<tr>
<td>$9 + 7 =$

$16 - 7 =$

$16 - 9 =$</td>
<td>If it is December 9, how many days is it until December 16?</td>
<td>$$\begin{array}{r} 224 \\ -\ 36 \\ \hline \end{array}$$</td>
</tr>
<tr>
<td>Erica had 25 cents. Loc gave her 36 cents. Now how much does Erica have?</td>
<td>The perimeter is 120 feet. How long is the bottom line?
50 ft
30 ft
20 ft</td>
<td>Rosa has 27 baseball cards. Alex has 40 baseball cards. How many more cards does Alex have than Rosa?</td>
</tr>
<tr>
<td>$$\begin{array}{r} 267 \\ 46 \\ +\ 35 \\ \hline \end{array}$$</td>
<td>How many inches are in 3 feet?</td>
<td>There are 3 rows of seats. There are 7 seats in each row. How many seats are in all 3 rows?</td>
</tr>
</table>

Name ____________________

Game 7

$5 + 9 =$ $14 - 5 =$ $14 - 9 =$	You have 5 points. How many more points do you need to have 14 points?	What number am I? I have 2 digits. I am an odd number. When you add my digits, you get 4. I am less than 25.
$\begin{array}{r} 59 \\ +\ 95 \\ \hline \end{array}$	What numbers come next? 10, 21, 32, 43, ____, ____	Together, Hana and Tim scored 14 points. Hana scored 6 points more than Tim. How many points did each person score?
How many inches are in 4 feet?	$\begin{array}{r} 95 \\ -\ 59 \\ \hline \end{array}$	Write an addition problem for this drawing. □□□□□ □□□□ □□□ ___ + ___ + ___ = ___

Name ______________________________

Game 8

$9 + 8 =$ $17 - 8 =$ $17 - 9 =$	Max runs 7 miles each week. How many miles does he run in 6 weeks?	98 $+ 89$
Unscramble this number name. tennevees (Hint: It is between 10 and 20.)	There are 4 quarts in 1 gallon. How many quarts are in 5 gallons?	Write the number five thousand, one hundred twelve.
98 $- 89$	Pedro runs 7 miles each week. How many weeks will it take him to run 28 miles?	What number am I? I am an odd number between 35 and 42. I am not the sum of 15 and 22. I am not the difference of 60 and 19.

Name ______________________________

Game 9

$9 + 4 =$ $13 - 4 =$ $13 - 9 =$	Write the word name for this number. Be sure to spell it correctly. 348	$\begin{array}{r} 1{,}394 \\ +\ 493 \\ \hline \end{array}$
How many hours are in 1 day?	How many legs do 7 elephants, 6 lions, 4 birds, and 1 snake have all together?	How many minutes are in 1 hour?
What numbers come next? 20, 18, 16, 14, 12, ____, ____	I have 2 quarters, 3 dimes, 2 nickels, and 4 pennies. How much money do I have?	What is the sum of 8, 7, and 6?

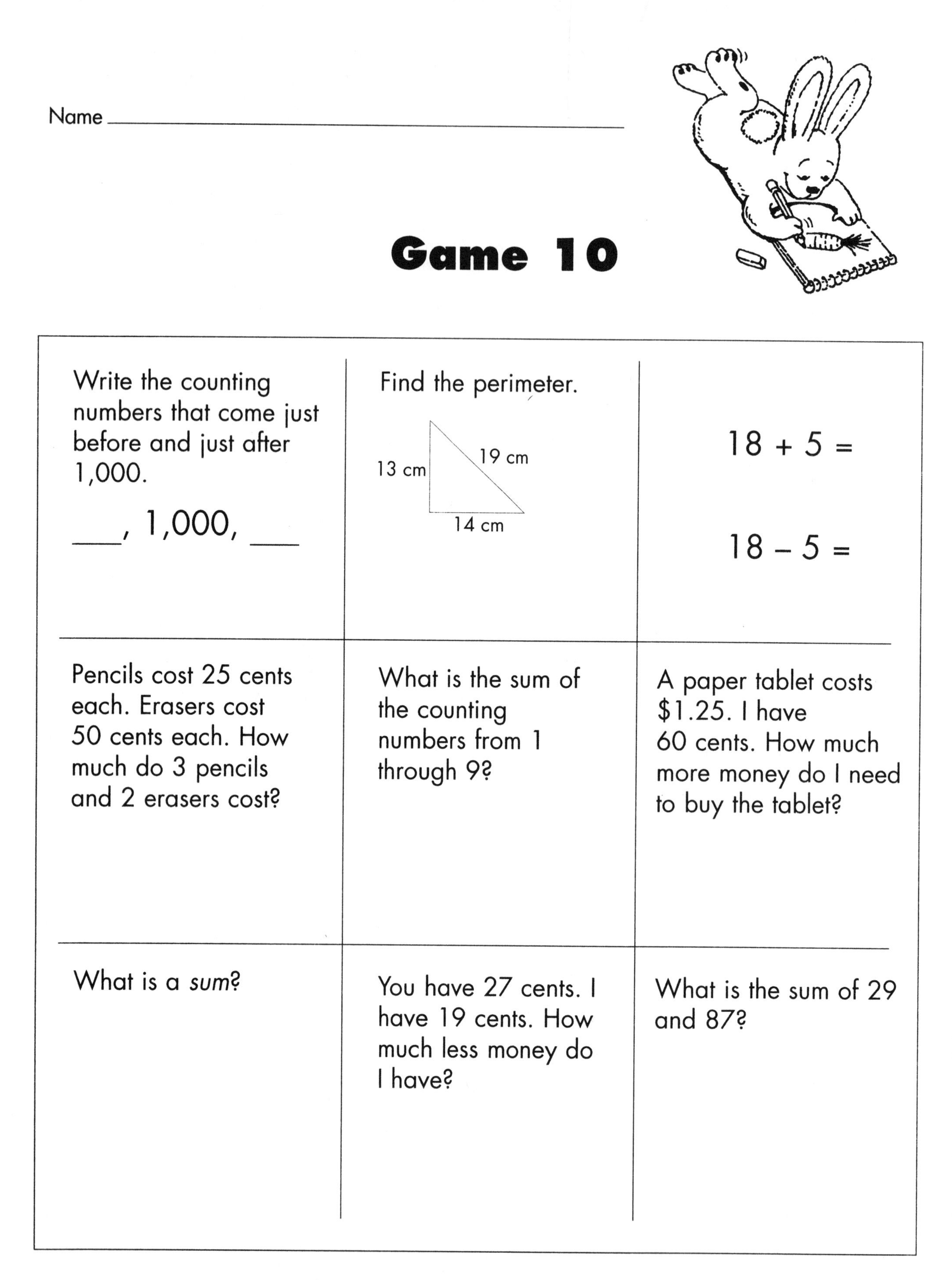

Name ____________________

Game 10

Write the counting numbers that come just before and just after 1,000. ___, 1,000, ___	Find the perimeter. 13 cm, 19 cm, 14 cm	18 + 5 = 18 – 5 =
Pencils cost 25 cents each. Erasers cost 50 cents each. How much do 3 pencils and 2 erasers cost?	What is the sum of the counting numbers from 1 through 9?	A paper tablet costs $1.25. I have 60 cents. How much more money do I need to buy the tablet?
What is a *sum*?	You have 27 cents. I have 19 cents. How much less money do I have?	What is the sum of 29 and 87?

Name ______________________________

Game 11

$13 + 4 = 25 - \square$	Write 7,026 in words. Be sure to spell correctly.	$16 + \square = 7 + 14$
10 onions cost a dollar. How much do 30 onions cost?	What number am I? I am between 10 and 20. The sum of my digits is 7.	Circle the tens digit. Underline the ones digit. 5,246
$22 - 13 = 3 + \square$	10 onions cost a dollar. How many onions can you buy for $5.00?	$14 + 6 = 11 + \square$

Name ______________________________

Game 12

9 + 6 = 15 – 6 = 15 – 9 =	Candy costs 25 cents for 3 pieces. How many pieces of candy can I buy for 50 cents?	18 + ☐ = 19 + 7
What number comes next? 15, 12, 9, ___	Errol has 69 cents. He has 2 quarters and 1 dime. The rest of his money is in pennies. How many pennies does he have?	7 cars stopped at school. 4 students stepped out of each car. How many students were there all together?
18 + 17 = 25 + ☐	If 3 pieces of candy cost 25 cents, how much do 9 pieces of candy cost?	4,502 – 853 _____

Name ______________________________

Game 13

<table>
<tr>
<td>

$7 + 5 =$

$12 - 5 =$

$12 - 7 =$

</td>
<td>The girls at the swimming pool had 30 toes in all. How many girls were there?</td>
<td>

$$\begin{array}{r} 75 \\ +\ 57 \\ \hline \end{array}$$

</td>
</tr>
<tr>
<td>Look at a calendar. List the months that have exactly 30 days.</td>
<td>What numbers do these Roman numerals represent?
X = ___
V = ___
IV = ___</td>
<td>How many days are in a year that is not a leap year?</td>
</tr>
<tr>
<td>What numbers come next?
1, 2, 1, 1, 2, 2,
1, 1, 1, ___,
___, ___</td>
<td>

$$\begin{array}{r} 356 \\ -\ 167 \\ \hline \end{array}$$

</td>
<td>How many months are in a year?</td>
</tr>
</table>

Name ______________________________

Game 14

Circle the tens digit. Underline the hundreds digit. 15,648	If it is 8:00 A.M. now, what time will it be in 7 hours?	How could you use the numbers 5, 8, and 2 to get a sum of 17? Use each number at least once.
1 dime equals how many nickels? 7 dimes equal how many nickels?	Fill in the boxes. $\begin{array}{r} 4\,\square \\ +\,\square\,3 \\ \hline 9\,4 \end{array}$	1 dime equals how many nickels? 12 nickels equal how many dimes?
$\begin{array}{r} 1{,}964 \\ +\,895 \\ \hline \end{array}$	What is the perimeter of this rectangle? 5 ft 7 ft	$\begin{array}{r} 1{,}964 \\ -\,845 \\ \hline \end{array}$

Name ______________________________

Game 15

$8 + 3 = \square$ $8 + \square = 11$ $\square + 8 = 11$	How many nickels equal 1 quarter? How many quarters equal 15 nickels?	$65 + 44 =$ $65 - 44 =$
Start with the number of days in a year that is not a leap year. Subtract the number of days in 2 weeks. How many days are left?	It takes $6\frac{1}{2}$ hours to roast a turkey. I want the turkey done at 6:00 P.M. When should I put it into the oven?	How many inches are in 1 foot? How many inches are in 4 feet?
$7 + 7 + 7 =$ $3 \times 7 =$	How many nickels equal 4 quarters?	$\begin{array}{r} 465 \\ 626 \\ +\ 81 \\ \hline \end{array}$

Name ______________________________

Game 16

$24 + 8 = \square$ $\square + 8 = 32$ $32 - \square = 24$	If I have 20 cents, how much more money do I need to make a dollar?	$\begin{array}{r} 137 \\ -\ 58 \\ \hline \end{array}$
A = 1 B = 2 C = 3 D = 4 If this pattern continues, how much is Z worth?	If today is Tuesday, what day was it 8 days ago?	$\begin{array}{r} \$6.38 \\ +\ 7.56 \\ \hline \end{array}$
Jo has 2 quarters, 1 dime, and 3 nickels. Al has 3 quarters, 2 dimes, and 2 nickels. How much should Al give Jo so they have the same amount?	What numbers come next? 25, 21, 17, 13, ___, ___	Mandisa was born on February 10, 1985. John was born on February 10, 1969. How many years older is John?

Name ________________________________

Game 17

$82 + 65 =$ ____	$40 + \square = 100$	$92 - 69 =$ ____
27 students are in third grade. 26 students are in fourth grade. How many students are in both grades?	A = 1, B = 2, C = 3, D = 4, and so on. The word *cab* is worth 6. How much is *zebra* worth?	What numbers come next? 6, 13, 16, 23, 26, ___, ___
The sum of the ages of Andy, Kintu, and Joe is 36. Andy is 9. Kintu is 14. How old is Joe?	$200 - \square = 107$	20 people are going to a picnic. How many cars are needed if 4 people can ride in each car?

Name ________________________________

Game 18

4 − 8 = ☐ ☐ + 8 = 14	How many pints are in 1 quart?	17 − 9 = ☐ 8 + ☐ = 17
Mansi bought 2 books for $1.39 each. She gave the clerk a 5 dollar bill. How much change did she get back?	The cars and bikes at my house have a total of 10 wheels. How many cars and bike are there? ___ cars ___ bikes	Mario paid $3.49 for a book. Jan bought a book for $2.59. How much more did Mario's book cost?
Lola can peel a potato in 2 minutes. How many potatoes can she peel in 10 minutes?	How much time passes from 8:00 A.M. until 10:15 A.M.? ____ hours and ____ minutes	6 + 6 + 6 = 6 x 3 ___

Name ______________________________

Game 19

Casey has $4.35, and I have $2.97. How much money do Casey and I have together?	What number comes next? 997, 998, 999, ____	Yoriko has $4.35 more than I have. I have $2.97. How much money does Yoriko have?
Find the missing digits. $$\begin{array}{r} 2\,\square\,7 \\ +\ \square\,7\,1 \\ \hline 5\,7\,8 \end{array}$$	I bought candy for $0.59 and gum for $0.25. How much money did I spend?	Ms. Kim drove 885 miles 1 week and 765 miles the next week. How many miles did she drive in the 2 weeks?
$$\begin{array}{r} 2{,}178 \\ -\ 1{,}259 \\ \hline \end{array}$$	When you subtract 9 from my number, you get 25. What is my number?	Write the next 4 even numbers. 0, ____, ____, ____, ____

Name ________________________________

Game 20

$9 + 9 =$ $18 - 9 =$	I have 1 dollar, 3 quarters, and 2 dimes. How much money do I have?	$\begin{array}{r} 118 \\ -\ 99 \\ \hline \end{array}$
I had 47 comic books. I gave Tom 28 of my comic books, and he gave me 15 of his. How many do I have now?	How many hours are in 2 days plus 7 hours?	$\begin{array}{r} 746 \\ 855 \\ +\ 64 \\ \hline \end{array}$
Round these numbers to the nearest hundred. 349 ____ 1,229 ____	If today is May 2, what will the date be 3 weeks from now?	How much time has passed from the first clock to the second?

Name ____

Game 21

$8 + 8 =$ $16 - 8 =$	How many inches are in 2 feet?	I had \$20.00. I spent \$2.50 for lunch, \$5.25 for a book, and \$3.75 for a movie. How much money do I have left?
I have 159 marbles in one box and 128 marbles in another. How many marbles are in the 2 boxes?	A team played 15 games. It won 3 games more than it lost. It won ____ games. It lost ____ games.	What is the value of 4 five dollar bills, 2 one dollar bills, 3 quarters, 1 nickel, and 2 pennies?
\$50.25 – 16.34 _______	What numbers come next? 0, 6, 12, 18, ____, ____	400 – 237 _______

Name ______________________________

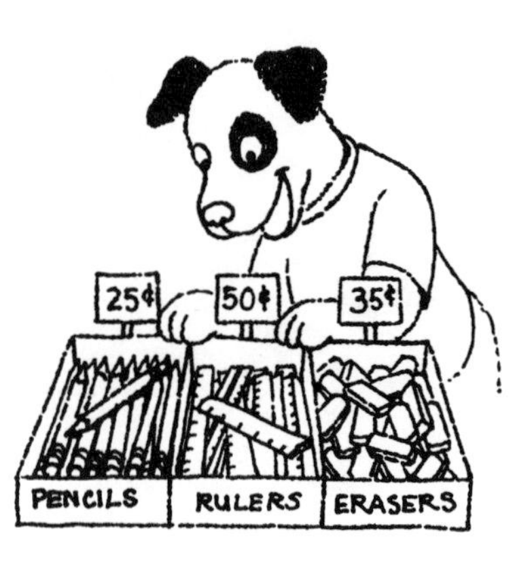

Game 22

$6 + 6 =$ $12 - 6 =$	Carlos had ten dollars. He spent three dollars and fifty cents playing video games and four dollars on comic books. How much does he have left?	$\begin{array}{r} 789 \\ +\ 43 \\ \hline \end{array}$
How many days are in three weeks?	The sum of two numbers is twenty-one. One number is nine more than the other. What are the numbers?	Write the number sixty thousand, eight hundred nine.
If this pattern continued, what would the twelfth shape look like? □ ▬ □ ▬ □ ▬	What numbers come next? 0, 8, 16, 24, ____, ____	Pencils cost twenty-five cents each. Erasers cost thirty-five cents each. Rulers cost fifty cents each. I spent one dollar and thirty-five cents on four things. What did I buy?

Name ____

Game 23

Write the number for twelve dollars and fifteen cents.	6 + 6 + 6 + 6 = 4 x 6 =	Draw the hands to show 3:45.
Underline the hundreds digit. Circle the thousands digit. 52,168	If it is now 9:30 A.M., how long will it be until lunch at noon?	Kala made 13 shots in a basketball game. She got 2 points for each shot. How many points did she score?
Name 9 coins that have a total value of 59 cents. ____ pennies ____ nickels ____ dimes ____ quarters	Write 9,804 in words. Be sure to spell correctly.	6,845 – 5,862 ______

Name ______________________________

Game 24

Write the number for four dollars and seventy cents.	7 + 7 + 7 + 7 =	A = 5 B = 10 C = 15 D = 20 Continue the pattern. What letter is worth 50?
4 x 7 =	If you write the numbers from 1 to 30, how many 2s do you write?	Jamie threw 12 darts and hit the target 7 times. She scored 3 points for each hit, and lost 2 points for each miss. What was her score?
Draw the hands to show 45 minutes after 8:30. 12 1 2 3 4 5 6 7 8 9 10 11	Write the number 37 in words. Be sure to spell correctly.	How many dimes equal 3 dollars?

Name ______________________________

Game 25

$7 + 7 =$ $14 - 7 =$	5 students shared 10 plums. Each student got the same number of plums. How many did each student get?	$4 + 4 + 4 =$ $4 \times 3 =$
Half of 10 is ____. Half of 16 is ____. Half of 12 is ____. Half of 18 is ____.	What number added to itself gives a sum of 50?	Marcos played 7 games. He scored 3 points in each game. How many points did he score all together?
21 boys divided into 3 teams. Each team had the same number of boys. How many boys were on each team?	What numbers come next? 0, 9, 18, 27, ____, ____	How many piles of 3 cards can be made from 21 cards?

Name ______________________________

Game 26

8 + 7 = 15 – 7 = 15 – 8 =	Carla runs eight miles each week. How many miles will she run in five weeks?	I am an even number between twenty-three and thirty. I am not four times seven. I am not seventeen plus seven. What number am I?
Unscramble this number name. dendruh	8 + 8 + 8 = 8 x 3 =	Write the number ten thousand, two hundred one.
Eight students collected twenty-four rocks. Each student collected the same number of rocks. How many rocks did each student collect?	Carla runs eight miles each week. How many weeks will it take her to run forty miles?	Three boys shared twenty-four dollars. They divided the money equally. How much money did each boy get?

Name ______________________________

Game 27

24 x 4 ____	Cross out the number that does not belong. 3 7 6 5 1 Explain your answer.	4 x 7 = 7 x 4 =
What is the tenth month of the year?	The fence around my yard is in the shape of a rectangle 22 feet long and 18 feet wide. What is the total length of my fence?	□ □ x 2 ____ 6 8
539 705 + 882 ____	I have 5 coins worth a total of 13 cents. What coins do I have?	4,003 – 606 ____

Name ________________________________

Game 28

How much greater is 9 + 8 than 7 + 6?	What is the difference of 64 and 46?	A box contains 18 cubes. Each cube is either red or blue. There are twice as many red cubes as blue cubes. How many blue cubes are in the box?
What is the sum of 64 and 46?	6 x 5 = 5 x 6 =	What is the product of 4 and 4?
1,548 2,073 + 514 _____	48 x 2 _____	100 – 69 _____

Name ______________________________

Game 29

How much greater is 9 + 7 than 6 + 5?	What number comes next? 2, 5, 9, 14, ___	$8 \times 6 =$ $6 \times 8 =$
There are 2 pints in 1 quart. How many pints are in 8 quarts?	Joey bought 7 apples and ate all but 3. How many apples were left?	The sum of 13 and 6 is _____. The difference of 13 and 6 is _____. The product of 13 and 6 is _____.
$\begin{array}{r} \$1.27 \\ +\ 8.48 \\ \hline \end{array}$	$\begin{array}{r} 183 \\ \times\ 5 \\ \hline \end{array}$	$\begin{array}{r} \$\ 8.27 \\ -\ 2.48 \\ \hline \end{array}$

Name ______________________________

Game 30

List the even numbers between 1 and 11.	Cross out the number that does not belong. 15 12 9 7 3 Explain your answer.	5 basketball players made 6 free throws each. How many free throws did they make all together?
Sue has 1 dollar, 2 nickels, and 3 pennies. How much more does she need to buy a book that costs $1.59?	$a - b = 3$ $a + b = 15$ $a =$ ___ $b =$ ___	It is now 3:15 P.M. What time will it be 4 hours and 15 minutes from now?
How much less is 10 + 10 than 6 x 5?	$2.98 + 3.49 ―――	How much greater is 10 x 10 than 39 + 26?

Name ______________________________

Game 31

4 x 8 = 8 x 4 =	It is now 10:30 A.M. What time will it be $3\frac{1}{2}$ hours from now?	What is 32 divided by 8? What is 32 divided by 4?
Circle the ten thousands digit. Underline the hundreds digit. 152,084	Use the numbers 1, 3, and 4 to write a problem with an answer of 12. Use each number once. Add, subtract, multiply, or divide.	What number comes next? 12, 24, 36, ____
How much less is 14 – 8 than 9 + 9?	Give the value of 5 nickels, 7 dimes, 2 quarters, and 3 pennies.	$\begin{array}{r} 6{,}927 \\ -\ 389 \\ \hline \end{array}$

Name ______________________________

Game 32

<table>
<tr>
<td>$7 \times 5 =$

$5 \times 7 =$</td>
<td>How many quarters equal 10 dollars?</td>
<td>What is 35 divided by 5?

What is 35 divided by 7?</td>
</tr>
<tr>
<td>What is a quotient?</td>
<td>List 3 pairs of numbers with a product of 12.
_____ and _____
_____ and _____
_____ and _____</td>
<td>The sum of 14 and 7 is _____.
The difference of 14 and 7 is _____.
The product of 14 and 7 is _____.
The quotient of 14 and 7 is _____.</td>
</tr>
<tr>
<td>How much greater is $17 + 26$ than 5×8?</td>
<td>My mom baked 3 dozen cookies just for me. I ate 6 cookies each day for 5 days. How many cookies were left?</td>
<td>$$\begin{array}{r} \$15.05 \\ +\ \ 7.20 \\ \hline \end{array}$$</td>
</tr>
</table>

Name ______________________________

Game 33

$7 \times 9 =$ $9 \times 7 =$	What is the sum of 397 and 246?	____ divided by 9 equals 7. ____ divided by 7 equals 9.
$\begin{array}{r} 43 \\ \times 7 \\ \hline \end{array}$	If it is 8:00 A.M. now, what time will it be in $4\frac{1}{2}$ hours?	$3\overline{)25}$
A can of tennis balls contains 3 balls. I need to buy 36 tennis balls. How many cans should I buy?	Tennis balls cost $2.98 per can. How much do 8 cans cost?	A can of tennis balls contains 3 balls. I bought 13 cans. How many balls did I get?

Name ________________________________

Game 34

9 x 6 = 6 x 9 =	One meter equals _______ centimeters. Four meters equal _______ centimeters.	Fifty-four divided by _________ equals six. Fifty-four divided by _________ equals nine.
Six students donated six books each. How many books did the students donate all together?	I have fewer than 20 cards. Put in piles of 4, two are left over. Put in piles of 3, two are left over. How many cards do I have?	$5\overline{)205}$
A grasshopper travels six inches with each jump. How many jumps will it make to travel four feet?	Six people each filled the same number of bags with trash. Forty-eight bags were filled. How many bags did each person fill?	1 foot = _____ inches 1 yard = _____ feet 1 yard = _____ inches

Name ______________________________

Game 35

$4 \times 7 =$ $7 \times 4 =$	I bought 6 dozen rolls for a party. How many rolls did I buy?	___ divided by 4 is 8. ___ divided by 8 is 4.
Circle the thousands digit. Underline the tens digit. 45,678	Estimate the width of the box around this problem. ________ Measure the width.	80 students are divided equally into 4 groups. How many students are in each group?
$6 \overline{)360}$	Estimate the width of the box around all the problems on this page. ________ Measure the width.	I bought 2 notebooks for \$0.89 each. I gave the clerk a 5 dollar bill. How much change did I get back?

Name ______________________________

Game 36

$9 \times 8 =$ $8 \times 9 =$	How many weeks are in 1 year?	What is 72 divided by 9? What is 72 divided by 8?
If May 4 is a Monday, list the dates of the other Mondays in May. May ____, May ____, and May ____	When I multiply my number by itself and then add 6, I get 22. What is my number?	If April 7 is a Tuesday, what day will April 15 be?
Ellie is 9 years old. How old will she be in 13 years?	$\begin{array}{r} 275 \\ \times\ 10 \\ \hline \end{array}$	Ellie is 9 years old. Her mother is 4 times as old. How old is Ellie's mother?

Name ______________________________

Game 37

9 x 4 = 4 x 9 =	Each day last week, I earned $10.00 more than I earned the day before. I earned $5.00 on Monday. How much did I earn on Friday?	36 divided by ___ is 9. 36 divided by ___ is 4.
I worked from Monday through Friday last week. Each day, I earned $10.00 more than I earned the day before. I earned $5.00 on Monday. How much did I earn for the entire week?	Complete the pattern. 1 2 3 4 5 6 _ _ _ _ What is the sum for the 10 numbers?	Write the number sixty thousand, three hundred two.
$5\overline{)667}$	Circle the ten thousands digit. Underline the hundreds digit. 45,789	Half of 24 is ____. Half of 18 is ____. Half of 30 is ____.

Name ______________________________

Game 38

A frog jumped 12 times, traveling 8 inches with each jump. How far did the frog travel all together? ____ inches, or ____ feet	Write the decimal number for one tenth.	A frog jumped 3 times, traveling the same distance with each jump. The frog traveled a total of 36 inches. How long was each jump? ___ inches, or ___ foot
$5.46 4.89 + 7.04 ______	I want to buy a bike that costs $125.00. I now have $48.00. How much more money do I need?	6,201 − 3,432 ______
A teacher divided 27 students into 3 groups. Each group had the same number of students. How many students were in each group?	608 x 37 ______	I have $8.45. You have twice as much money as I have. How much money do you have?

Name ______________________________

Game 39

40 cars are parked in 8 rows. Each row has the same number of cars. How many cars are in each row?	Write a fraction for 0.9. $\frac{\square}{\square}$	There are 8 rows of 40 cars in a parking lot. How many cars are in the parking lot all together?
Write four and five tenths as a decimal number.	$\begin{array}{r} 3.8 \\ +\ 4.6 \\ \hline \end{array}$	How many meters are in a kilometer?
There were 321 cars in a parking lot. 177 of the cars left at noon. How many cars remained in the lot?	Write 6.4 in words.	A parking lot holds 430 cars. It is half full. How many cars are in the lot?

Name ______________________________

Game 40

Cindy is reading a 200-page book. She read 35 pages Monday, 26 pages Tuesday, and 17 pages Wednesday. How many pages are left to read?	Name the sixth month of the year. How many days are in the sixth month?	What is the sum of the first 5 odd numbers?
What is the sum of the first 7 whole numbers, starting with 0?	How much more is the product of 9 and 3 than the sum of 9 and 3?	Adra bought a football for \$31.95, and 2 baseballs for \$19.00 each. How much did she spend in all?
It took me 30 minutes to type 1 page. At this rate, how many hours will it take me to type 4 pages?	It is now 3:00 P.M. What time will it be $4\frac{1}{2}$ hours from now?	How many half dollars equal a 10 dollar bill?

Name ______________________________

Game 41

What does the word *perimeter* mean?	What is the perimeter of this rectangle? 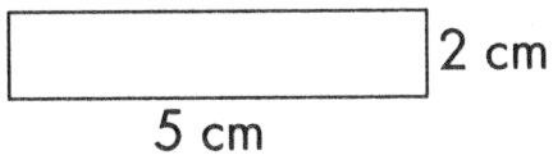 	What is the perimeter of this square? 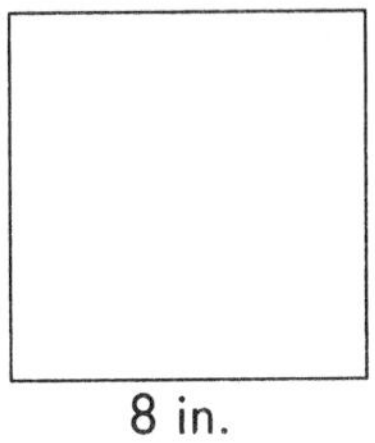
Unscramble this number name. dosutahn	I earn \$1.00 the first hour I work, \$3.00 the second hour, \$5.00 the third hour, and so on. How much will I earn in an 8-hour work day?	Multiply the hundred thousands digit by the hundreds digit. 1,234,567 ☐ x ☐ = ☐
Cross out the number that does not belong. 12 8 10 4 16 Explain your answer.	$\begin{array}{r} 308 \\ -\ 59 \\ \hline \end{array}$	$8\overline{)702}$

Name ______________________________

Game 42

$9 \times 8 =$ $9 + 8 =$	What is the value of 3 quarters, 5 dimes, 7 nickels, and 4 pennies?	$\begin{array}{r} 36 \\ \times 9 \\ \hline \end{array}$
The perimeter of this square is 16 inches. [square] What is the length of each side?	A = 1, B = 2, C = 3, D = 4, and so on. What is the sum of the letters in the word *teacher*?	The perimeter of this rectangle is 16 feet. [rectangle] 3 ft How long is the bottom edge?
What is the perimeter of this square? [square] 2.1 cm	$\begin{array}{r} 2.4 \\ 2.4 \\ 2.4 \\ + 2.4 \\ \hline \end{array}$	How much less is the sum of 8 and 7 than the product of 8 and 7?

Name ______________________________

Game 43

Write 4 different number sentences using the numbers 1, 15, 7, 8. ☐ + ☐ = ☐ ☐ + ☐ = ☐ ☐ − ☐ = ☐ ☐ − ☐ = ☐	Ling has 17 crayons. His sister has twice as many. How many crayons does Ling's sister have?	9 8 7 6 + 5 ———
Describe the rule for this number pattern. 0, 3, 6, 9, 12, 15	Today is Tuesday, September 21. What will be the day and the date 11 days from now?	Circle the number that has a 9 in the millions place. 4,109,325 9,816,290 3,921,456 91,234,567
Circle 2 numbers with a sum of 15. 8 5 6 9 4 3	I have 17 crayons. You have twice as many as I have. How many crayons do we have all together?	List all the 3-digit numbers that could be made from the digits 1, 2, and 3. Do not repeat a digit in a number.

Name ______________________________

Game 44

If △ + 9 = 17, then △ = ___ If 17 − ◯ = 8, then ◯ = ___	What number comes next? 12, 24, 36, 48, ___	3 9 2 6 + 4 ___
Describe the rule for this number pattern. 1, 5, 9, 13, 17, 21	I earn $1.00 the first hour I work, $2.00 the second hour, $3.00 the third hour, and so on. How much will I earn in 10 hours?	Round 465 to the nearest ten. Round 465 to the nearest hundred.
Circle 2 numbers with a difference of 9. 1 5 7 5 8 16 3 11	List all the 2-digit numbers that can be made from the digits 2, 4, and 6. Do not repeat a digit in a number.	3,648 + 2,503 ___

Name ________________________________

Game 45

How much more 8 + 8 than 7 + 6?	I have 27 grapes. You have twice that many. How many grapes do you have? How many grapes do we have together?	2,356 – 507 ____
I have 50 stickers. You have half that many. How many stickers do you have? How many stickers do we have together?	Today is Monday, August 16. What will be the day and the date 18 days from now?	Circle the number that has a 2 in the ten thousands place. 2,134,567 1,234,567 3,412,567 4,827,301
What number comes next? 32, 28, 24, 20, ___	The temperature is 71 degrees Fahrenheit. It is 18 degrees cooler than it was yesterday. What was the temperature yesterday?	25 15 7 + 24 ____

Name ______________________________

Game 46

Write 4 number sentences using the numbers 13, 7, and 6.

□ + □ = □

□ + □ = □

□ − □ = □

□ − □ = □

What time will it be 3 hours and 14 minutes from the time on this clock?

How many grams are in a kilogram?

How many grams are in 7 kilograms?

Estimate the sum by rounding each number to the nearest hundred.

$$\begin{array}{r} 107 \\ 922 \\ 451 \\ +\ 527 \\ \hline \end{array}$$

What number am I? I am between 3 and 10. I am not 2 x 4. I am not 17 – 13.

Write the number nine thousand, two.

Unscramble this number name.

wytent

$$\begin{array}{r} 945 \\ 2{,}618 \\ +\ \ 97 \\ \hline \end{array}$$

Tina has $2.50 in nickels. How many nickels does she have?

Name ____

Game 47

If △ + 6 = 14, then
△ = ____
 	
If 14 – ○ = 8, then
○ = ____
	Cross out the number that does not belong.
	1 7 4 3 9
	Explain your answer.
		Carlita runs 6 miles each week. How far will she run in 5 weeks?

What is a *polygon*?	$\begin{array}{r} 26 \\ \times\ 5 \\ \hline \end{array}$	How much less is 12 – 7 than 8 x 3?
Carlita runs 6 miles each week. How many weeks will it take her to run 18 miles?	Circle the number that has a 0 in the thousands place. 3,234,560 1,432,056 1,230,456 2,041,561	A triangle has ___ sides. A square has ___ sides. A parallelogram has ___ sides. A pentagon has ___ sides.

Name ____________________________________

Game 48

How much more is 9 + 7 than 8 + 6?	Write the number for eleven dollars and eleven cents.	Five boys have thirty pieces of candy to share equally. How many pieces will each boy get?
A box contains eighty-four marbles. Forty-eight are blue. How many are not blue?	What rule changes each first number to the second? 17 → 10 20 → 13 9 → 2 15 → 8	How many quarts are in a gallon? How many quarts are in two gallons? How many quarts are in ten gallons?
Each number is 6 more than the previous number. Write the next four numbers below. 0, 6, ___, ___ ___, ___	What is the perimeter of this rectangle? (rectangle: 6 by 7)	60 x 70 ___

Name ______________________________

Game 49

<table>
<tr>
<td>Write 4 number sentences using the numbers 12, 5, and 7.
□ + □ = □
□ + □ = □
□ − □ = □
□ − □ = □</td>
<td>Name the eighth month of the year.

How many days does the eighth month have?</td>
<td>$$\begin{array}{r} 36 \\ \times\ 6 \\ \hline \end{array}$$</td>
</tr>
<tr>
<td>What does area mean?

What is the area of this rectangle?

4 ft
6 ft</td>
<td>Name 6 coins that have a total value of 36 cents.
____ dimes
____ nickels
____ pennies</td>
<td>How many ounces are in 1 pound?

How many ounces are in 5 pounds?</td>
</tr>
<tr>
<td>$6\overline{)246}$</td>
<td>Write the next 6 numbers.
0, 7, 14, 21, 28,
____, ____, ____,
____, ____, ____</td>
<td>$$\begin{array}{r} 5{,}204 \\ -\ 3{,}315 \\ \hline \end{array}$$</td>
</tr>
</table>

Name ______________________________

Game 50

<table>
<tr>
<td>☐ x 8 = 56

56 ÷ 8 = ☐

☐ x 7 = 56

56 ÷ 7 = ☐</td>
<td>Ann has 126 cards. Pat has twice as many. How many cards does Pat have?

How many cards do Ann and Pat have together?</td>
<td>What numbers come next?

63, 56, 49, 42,

____, ____, ____, ____</td>
</tr>
<tr>
<td>Omar has 126 cards. Lani has half as many. How many cards does Lani have?

How many cards do Omar and Lani have together?</td>
<td>I am thinking of 2 numbers with a difference of 8 and a product of 20. What are the numbers?</td>
<td>743
957
82
+ 6
____</td>
</tr>
<tr>
<td>How many pennies equal $4.00?</td>
<td>Circle the number that has a 4 in the ten thousands place.

6,472,103
4,890,123
3,149,567
2,074,135</td>
<td>805
x 23
____</td>
</tr>
</table>

Name ______________________________

Game 51

Write 4 number sentences using the numbers 9, 8, and 17. ☐ + ☐ = ☐ ☐ + ☐ = ☐ ☐ − ☐ = ☐ ☐ − ☐ = ☐	Unscramble this number name. ntenniee	$7\overline{)1{,}428}$
$9 \times 3 = 17 + \square$	What number am I? I am an odd number between 4 and 10. I am not 3 x 3, and I am not 13 – 8.	Write the number one thousand, forty-two.
How much less is 6 x 3 than 7 x 7?	Luis runs 9 miles each week. How many weeks will it take him to run 45 miles?	Luis runs 9 miles each week. How many miles will he run in 45 weeks?

Name ______________________________

Game 52

<table>
<tr>
<td>Write 4 number sentences using the numbers 9, 6, and 15.
□ + □ = □
□ + □ = □
□ − □ = □
□ − □ = □</td>
<td>$6\overline{)90}$</td>
<td>1 foot equals 12 inches. How many inches are in 6 feet?</td>
</tr>
<tr>
<td>$\begin{array}{r} 900 \\ -\ 273 \\ \hline \end{array}$</td>
<td>Sara saves 75 cents each week. How many weeks will it take her to save $3.00?</td>
<td>$\begin{array}{r} 76 \\ \times\ 5 \\ \hline \end{array}$</td>
</tr>
<tr>
<td>The cows and chickens on Peg's farm have a total of 10 legs. How many cows and chickens does Peg have?</td>
<td>$\begin{array}{r} \$79.18 \\ +\ 23.82 \\ \hline \end{array}$</td>
<td>Sara saves 75 cents each week. How much money will she save in 10 weeks?</td>
</tr>
</table>

Name ____________________________________

Game 53

4 ft 8 ft area = perimeter =	Lars had 47 comic books. Pam gave him 18 of her comic books, and he gave her 24 of his. Now how many comic books does Lars have?	Cross out the number that does not belong. 10 12 15 13 Explain your answer.
Circle the tens digit. Underline the millions digit. 1,234,567	$n \times n = 36$ $n + n = 12$ What does $n - n$ equal?	What is 12,365 rounded to the nearest hundred? ten? thousand?
Continue the pattern. 72, 64, 56, 48, ___, ___, ___, ___, ___	Jason has 75 comic books. Each book has 24 pages. How many pages are there all together?	Ramon has \$12.50. He wants to buy a book that costs \$16.98. How much more money does he need?

Name ______________________________

Game 54

Circle the numbers that have a sum of 35. 26 17 14 18	$5\overline{)100}$	Circle the numbers that have a difference of 7. 13 9 15 20 18
$8.67 – 5.79	How much more is 9 x 5 than 17 + 14?	9,035 x 6
5 students got off the school bus at the first stop, 7 at the second stop, and 10 at the third stop. 12 students remained on the bus. How many students did the bus start with?	674 839 + 54	If 3 apples cost 60 cents, how much do 9 apples cost?

Name ______________________________

Game 55

Circle the numbers that have a product of 81. 10 9 5 9 8 7	$3\overline{)924}$	There are 4 quarts in one gallon. How many quarts are in 10 gallons? How many quarts are in 12 gallons?
$\begin{array}{r} 603 \\ -\ 168 \\ \hline \end{array}$	Name 6 coins that have a value of 43 cents. ____ quarters ____ dimes ____ nickels ____ pennies	How much less is the product of 5 and 6 than the sum of 17 and 16?
In a basketball game, Al made 9 shots worth 2 points each and 3 free throws worth 1 point each. How many points did Al score?	$\begin{array}{r} 215 \\ \times\ 76 \\ \hline \end{array}$	Write 4 number sentences using the numbers 4, 9, and 13. ☐ + ☐ = ☐ ☐ + ☐ = ☐ ☐ − ☐ = ☐ ☐ − ☐ = ☐

Name ______________________________

Game 56

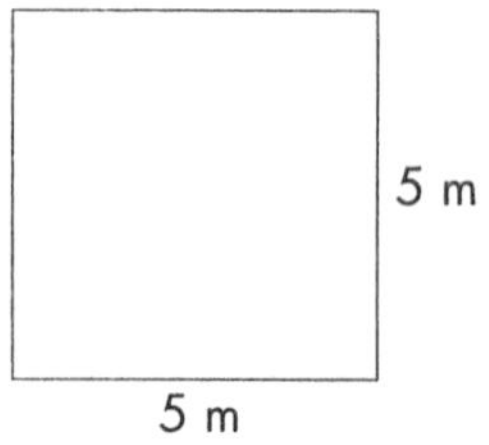 area = perimeter =	The temperature is 72 degrees Fahrenheit. Last night, it was 55 degrees. How much warmer is it now?	What numbers come next? 1, 1, 2, 3, 5, 8, ___, ___, ___, ___, ___
76 x 2 =	Today is Monday, June 5. What will be the day and date 30 days from now?	$2\overline{)76}$
Jeff has 76 cents. Amy has twice that much. How much does Amy have? How much money do they have together?	The temperature is 72 degrees Fahrenheit. It was 8 degrees cooler yesterday. What was the temperature yesterday?	I am thinking of 2 numbers. When you multiply them, you get 20. When you subtract them, you get 19. What are the 2 numbers?

Name ______________________________

Game 57

The sum of 8 and 4 is ___. The difference of 8 and 4 is ___. The product of 8 and 4 is ___. The quotient of 8 and 4 is ___.	$4 \times \square = 24$ $3 \times \square = 21$ $8 \times \square = 72$ $6 \times \square = 42$	I have 30 pencils. You have half as many. How many pencils do you have? How many pencils do we have together?
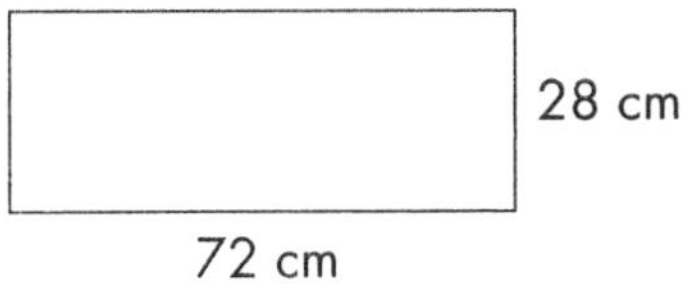 area = perimeter =	What number am I? If you multiply me by 6, then add 4, you get 58.	$\begin{array}{r} \$10.48 \\ -\ 8.57 \\ \hline \end{array}$
Write the number 0.3 in words.	Write the number five hundredths as a decimal number.	Write 4 number sentences using the numbers 5, 7, and 12. $\square + \square = \square$ $\square + \square = \square$ $\square - \square = \square$ $\square - \square = \square$

Name ______________________

Game 58

☐ x 5 = 35 35 ÷ 5 = ☐ ☐ x 7 = 35 35 ÷ 7 = ☐	I earn $5.00 each week for doing chores. How much will I earn in a year? (A year has 52 weeks.)	700 x 80
\$21.45 – 12.56	Beth walked 4 kilometers each day for 20 days. What total distance did she walk?	Boris walked 20 kilometers in 4 days. He walked the same distance each day. How far did he walk each day?
Fill in the boxes with the digits 2, 3, 8, and 9 to make the greatest possible product. ☐☐☐ X ☐	What is 2,085 rounded to the nearest ten? hundred?	9 x 4 = 20 + ☐

Name ______________________________

Game 59

<table>
<tr>
<td>The sum of 64 and 8 is ___.
The difference of 64 and 8 is ___.
The product of 64 and 8 is ___.
The quotient of 64 and 8 is ___.</td>
<td>Double 16.
Add 8.
Cut the result in half.
Multiply by five.</td>
<td>Nathan is three feet eight inches tall. His sister is three inches taller. How tall is Nathan's sister?</td>
</tr>
<tr>
<td>Write 2,035,104 in words. Be sure to spell correctly.</td>
<td>$6\overline{)42}$</td>
<td>Fill in the boxes with the digits 1, 2, 3, 4, and 5 to make the smallest possible answer.
□ □ □
– □ □
______</td>
</tr>
<tr>
<td>It rained a half inch on Monday and one and a half inches on Tuesday. How much rain fell during those two days?</td>
<td>357
x 9
____</td>
<td>Nita has seven dollars and fifty cents. She shares the money equally with her brother. How much money does each get?</td>
</tr>
</table>

Name ______________________________

Game 60

I am thinking of 2 numbers with a sum of 11 and a difference of 3. What are the 2 numbers?	Pens cost $1.19 each. Pencils cost $0.27 each. How much more does a pen cost than a pencil? How much do a pen and a pencil cost together?	I am thinking of 2 numbers with a sum of 12 and a product of 32. What are the 2 numbers?
18 ft 8 ft perimeter = area =	Unscramble this number name. lomlini	940 76 + 39 ———
I am thinking of 2 numbers with a quotent of 4 and a sum of 10. What are the 2 numbers?	Underline the tenths digit. Circle the hundredths digit. 452.78	What is 4,809 rounded to the nearest ten? hundred? thousand?

Name ______________________________

Game 61

<table>
<tr>
<td>Together, Pam and Lee have $15.00. Pam has twice as much as Lee. How much does Lee have?</td>
<td>$7\overline{)49}$</td>
<td>The sum of 9 and 3 is ___.
The difference of 9 and 3 is ___.
The product of 9 and 3 is ___.
The quotient of 9 and 3 is ___.</td>
</tr>
<tr>
<td>$\begin{array}{r} \square\,\square \\ -\ \ 9 \\ \hline 1\ \ 8 \end{array}$</td>
<td>I counted the legs on 10 cows and 5 ducks. How many more cow legs did I count than duck legs?</td>
<td>$\begin{array}{r} 76 \\ \times\ 8 \\ \hline \end{array}$</td>
</tr>
<tr>
<td>30 students went on a field trip. 3 students rode in each car. How many cars were needed?</td>
<td>Write 24.32 in words. Be sure to spell correctly.</td>
<td>30 students are going on a field trip. If 4 students can ride in each car, how many cars are needed?</td>
</tr>
</table>

Name ______________________________

Game 62

Which of these represents the greatest number? XII 17 5 x 3 12 + 6 32 – 18	$9.49 – 6.72 ______	Which of these represents the least number? IV 4 x 2 1 + 1 99 – 98 a dozen
Add these amounts: 5 cents, 26 cents, $1.19, 54 cents, and $3.55.	Unscramble this number name. ehigeten	302 302 – 89 + 89 ____ ____
$7\overline{)63}$ $7\overline{)630}$ $7\overline{)6,300}$	A lamp was priced at $50.00. Now it is on sale for 50% off. How much does the lamp cost now? (50% means half.)	If . . . 1 + 1 + 1 = 3 2 + 2 + 2 = 6 3 + 3 + 3 = 9 4 + 4 + 4 = 12 then . . . ☐ + ☐ + ☐ = 36

Name ______________________________

Game 63

$3\overline{)\square\square}$ with quotient 2 1	If milk costs $1.69 per gallon, how much do 2 gallons cost?	$\square5 + 4\square = 98$
Find the average of these numbers. 16 24 5	hamburger $0.85 bag of fries $0.80 soda pop $0.75 What do 2 burgers, 2 bags of fries, and 2 sodas cost?	How many inches are in 7 feet? How many feet are in 144 inches?
$32 - \square = 27$	Nadia is 10 years old. Her brother is 5 years old. How old will Nadia's brother be when Nadia is 18 years old?	$26 \times \square = 52$

Name ______________________________

Game 64

52 – ☐ = 13 13 + ☐ = 52	9 commercials are shown during a half-hour of T.V. How many commercials are shown during an hour and a half?	\$3.72 – 1.74 ______
How many months are in 3 years? How many years is 60 months?	How much more is 9 + 7 than 19 – 17?	Write 1,068 in words. Be sure to spell correctly.
1 + 2 = 3 1 + 2 + 3 = 6 1 + 2 + 3 + 4 = 10 Continue this pattern. What numbers add to 28?	19 x 7 ____	Circle the rectangles.

Name ______________________________

Game 65

<table>
<tr>
<td>In 4 games, Julie scored the following points.
game 1: 12 points
game 2: 6 points
game 3: 8 points
game 4: 14 points
What was her average?</td>
<td>385
− 96
____</td>
<td>65
+ 78
____</td>
</tr>
<tr>
<td>List the even numbers between 31 and 41.
___, ___, ___,
___, ___</td>
<td>16
x 8
____</td>
<td>List the odd numbers between 30 and 40.
___, ___, ___,
___, ___</td>
</tr>
<tr>
<td>A frog ate 5 bugs one day, 10 bugs the next day, 15 the third day, and so on. On what day did the frog eat 45 bugs?</td>
<td>Juan bought a book for $7.95 and 3 comics for $2.25 each. He gave the cashier a 20 dollar bill. How much change did he get?</td>
<td>987
654
+ 321
____</td>
</tr>
</table>

Name ______________________________

Game 66

68 + 57 ———	A pen costs $1.98. A pencil costs $0.33. How much more does 1 pen cost than 2 pencils?	204 – 85 ———
The sum of 2 numbers is 19. Their difference is 5. What are the numbers?	Cam is 11. He has twin younger sisters. When you add the ages of all 3 children, you get 21. How old are the twins?	Unscramble this number name. ysvtnee
37 x 46 ———	Lin wants to buy a stereo that costs $450.00. She has saved $278.00 so far. How much more money does she need?	$6\overline{)804}$

Name ________________ ____________

Game 67

<table>
<tr>
<td>9
x ☐
—
5 4</td>
<td>I am thinking of a number. If you divide my number by 2, you get 8. What do you get if you multiply my number by 2?</td>
<td>What could this mean?
1 y____ =
12 m____</td>
</tr>
<tr>
<td>3 7 ☐
+ 1 ☐ 9
—
5 1 0</td>
<td>Of all the pairs of numbers that add to 12, what pair has the greatest product?</td>
<td>4 2 ☐
+ 1 ☐ 9
—
3 0 9</td>
</tr>
<tr>
<td>6)54

9)54</td>
<td>Write the number four million, two hundred thousand, thirteen.</td>
<td>I have 9 coins with a total value of 25 cents. What coins do I have?
____ pennies
____ nickels
____ dimes</td>
</tr>
</table>

Name ____________________________________

Game 68

Solve 319 x 5 to find the year Pocahontas was born.	The Walt Disney Company made a movie about Pocahontas in MCMXCV. What year was that?	Divide 176 by 8 to find how long Pocahontas lived.
If Pocahontas was alive today, how old would she be?	A = 1, B = 2, C = 3, D = 4, and so on. What is the sum of the letters in *Pocahontas*?	Pocahontas married John Rolfe. Divide 38 by 2 to find out how old she was when she got married.
To find the year Pocahontas visited London, England, subtract 376 from 1992.	Start with 12. Double it. Now add 8. Cut the answer in half. Multiply that result by 5. Write the final answer.	What number does the Roman numeral XXI represent?

Name ______________________________

Game 69

<table>
<tr>
<td>The sum of 9 and 3 is ___.
The difference of 9 and 3 is ___.
The product of 9 and 3 is ___.
The quotient of 9 and 3 is ___.</td>
<td>35.85
+ 8.55
______</td>
<td>Multiply the number of days in June by the number of days in 2 weeks. Then add the number of months in a year. What is the answer?</td>
</tr>
<tr>
<td>What rule changes each first number to the second?
6 → 48
4 → 32
2 → 16</td>
<td>Find the average of these numbers.
55 95 62 28</td>
<td>What is 3 times 15?
What is $\frac{1}{3}$ of 15?</td>
</tr>
<tr>
<td>The original price of a flashlight was $12.96. It was marked down 50%. What did it cost?</td>
<td>Circle the thousandths digit.
Underline the hundredths digit.
1.023</td>
<td>How many inches are in 1 yard?
How many inches are in 11 yards?</td>
</tr>
</table>

Name ________________________________

Game 70

<table>
<tr>
<td>The sum of 6 and 9 is ___.

The difference of 6 and 9 is ___.

The product of 6 and 9 is ___.</td>
<td>What does probability mean?</td>
<td>A bag contains 10 marbles. 5 are red and 5 are blue. I reach in and take a marble. What is the probability that my marble is red?</td>
</tr>
<tr>
<td>$$\begin{array}{r} 34 \\ \times\ 9 \\ \hline \end{array}$$</td>
<td>Figure out the rule, and use it to to fill in the blank.

6 → 54
2 → 18
12 → 108
☐ → 9</td>
<td>$$\begin{array}{r} 3,\ 7\ 1\ 9 \\ +\ \square\ \square\ \square\ \square \\ \hline 6,\ 3\ 9\ 7 \end{array}$$</td>
</tr>
<tr>
<td>Identify the specified digits.

123.456

tenths _____
tens _____
hundredths _____
hundreds _____</td>
<td>What is 56,478 rounded to the nearest

thousand?

ten?</td>
<td>Estimate 369 x 9 by rounding 369 to the nearest hundred and 9 to the nearest ten.</td>
</tr>
</table>

Name ______________________________

Game 71

Which of these represents the greatest number? XVII 8 x 3 33 – 16 13 + 8 3 dozen 12 ÷ 2	9 x ☐ = 72 72 ÷ ☐ = 8	Which of these represents the least number? 13 – 8 12 – 3 9 x 2 7 + 5 VII half of 12
Circle 3 numbers that add to 23. 15 3 6 12 1 10 8 4	Continue the pattern. 1, 2, 4, 8, 16, ___, ___, ___, ___, ___ What is the sum of the 10 numbers?	Circle 3 numbers that have a product of 30. 8 5 2 4 9 3 1 10
What words come next? second, minute, hour, ______, ______, ______, ______	8 x ☐ = 32 32 ÷ ☐ = 8	What word comes next? ounce, cup, pint, ______

Name ______________________________

Game 72

Show where one-fourth would be located. 0 ——— 1	Identify the specified digits. 8,765,432.19 millions ___ tenths ___ thousands ___ ten thousands ___	Add the number of quarts in a gallon to the number of inches in a yard. Subtract the number of feet in a yard. Add the number of hours in a week.
How much more is eight times seven than six times nine?	List the first eight multiples of seven.	Find the average of these numbers. 28 46 71 39
Double 75. Add 8. Subtract 14. Divide by 9.	Multiply the number of ounces in a pound by the number of pints in a quart.	Eric had sixty-one dollars. He bought a CD for nine dollars and seventy-eight cents. How much money does he have left?

Name ______________________________

Game 73

Shade in three tenths of this drawing. 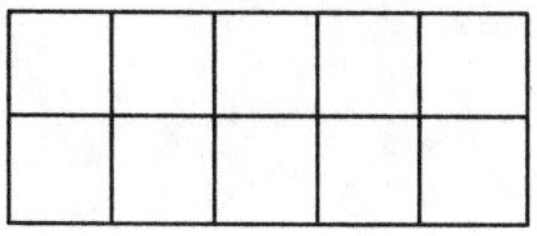 Write three tenths as a decimal number.	The largest freshwater fish is the sturgeon. The largest sturgeon ever caught weighed 2,860 pounds. About how many tons is this?	Your heart beats about 72 times each minute. About how many times will it beat in 1 day?
5.7 + 3.62 + 9.03 =	If today is Tuesday, what day will it be 50 days from now?	What rule changes each first number to the second? 6 → 42 4 → 28 7 → 49
Multiply the millions digit by the hundredths digit. 9,876,543.21 □ x □ = □	$\begin{array}{r} 0.57 \\ \times\ 0.3 \\ \hline \end{array}$	Write the first 8 multiples of 9.

Name ______________________________

Game 74

Write the word name for the number 5.43.	$\frac{1}{2} + \frac{1}{2} =$	Round 7.47 to the nearest tenth.
Write $\frac{2}{4}$ in lowest terms.	I have \$0.65 in quarters, dimes, and nickels. How many ways can this happen if I have at least 1 of each coin?	3.5 m; 6.5 m perimeter = area =
What does n equal? $\frac{3}{4} = \frac{12}{n}$	How many seconds are in 1 hour? How many seconds are in 1 day?	$\square + 2.5 = 3.8$

Name ____

Game 75

Draw a radius. ◯ Draw a diameter. ◯	What is the perimeter of this triangle? (2.5 m, 1.8 m, 4.1 m)	I have 80 cents in nickels and dimes. I have twice as many nickels as dimes. How many nickels do I have? How many dimes do I have?
Identify the specified digits. 8,123.4567 hundreds ____ thousandths ____ hundredths ____ thousands ____	4 people shook hands with each other once. How many handshakes was this?	A = 1, B = 2, C = 3, D = 4, and so on. What word do these numbers represent? 13 1 20 8
What rule changes each first number to the second? 6 → 36, 4 → 16, 2 → 4, 9 → 81	Fill in the blanks without repeating any numbers. ☐ x ☐ = 24, ☐ x ☐ = 24, ☐ x ☐ = 24, ☐ x ☐ = 24	A factor is a whole number that divides into another number with no remainder. List the 8 factors of 24.

Name ______________________________

Game 76

Define the word *factor.*	Write the word name for this number. 1,201.45	If 2 pounds of nuts costs \$4.30, how much does 1 pound of nuts cost? How much do 3 pounds of nuts cost?
Round 2.198 to the nearest tenth.	List the first 7 multiples of 8.	How much more is \$3.05 than \$1.87?
I am thinking of 2 numbers. If you add them, you get 15. If you multiply them, you get 36. What are the 2 numbers?	Unscramble this math word. pemutill	What rule changes each first number to the second? 15 → 3 35 → 7 60 → 12 100 → 20

Name ______________________________

Game 77

How much less is $0.65 than $1.04?	Identify the specified digits. 7,042.56 tenths ____ thousands ____ hundredths ____ ones ____	Multiply the number of days in December by the number of inches in 5 feet.
Multiply 8 by 7. Subtract 6. Divide by 10. Add 13. Divide by 3. What is the final answer?	I am thinking of an odd number between 15 and 30. It is a multiple of 3, and when you add its digits, you get 3. What is my number?	The sum of 12 and 6 is ___. The difference of 12 and 6 is ___. The product of 12 and 6 is ___. The quotient of 12 and 6 is ___.
List all six 3-digit numbers that have the digits 5, 9, and 4. ____, ____, ____, ____, ____, ____	How much more is 9 x 7 than 8 x 6?	What rule changes each first number to the second? 12 → 6 18 → 9 30 → 15

Name ______________________________

Game 78

$$\begin{array}{r} 1\ 3\ 7 \\ +\ \square\ \square\ \square \\ \hline 5\ 0\ 9 \end{array}$$	My pumpkin was 18 inches tall. When I told my friend about it, I said it was 1 foot and 6 inches tall. Did I tell the truth?	A bag contains 5 quarters and 1 nickel. If I reach in the bag and draw the first coin I touch, what is the probability that I will draw the nickel?
Find the average of these numbers. 12 8 16 4	$\frac{1}{2}$ of a dollar is \$0.50. How much is $\frac{1}{4}$ of a dollar?	4 friends divided 1 dollar equally. How much money did each friend get?
I bought 10 pounds of cat food for \$1.29 per pound. How much did I pay? I paid with a \$20.00 bill. How much change did I get?	How much greater is 27 x 3 than 9 x 9?	Is 0 a whole number? Is 0 a counting number?

Name ______________________________________

Game 79

Write the word name for 4.06.	Circle the largest number in each pair. 52.9 or 52.89 21.6 or 21.58	Write the decimal number for six and two hundredths.
Shade three fifths of the squares. □□□ □□□□ □□□	Mr. and Mrs. Jones have seven daughters. Each daughter has one brother. What is the number of people in the Jones family?	What is one third of twenty-four?
There are thirty days in April. If it rained two fifths of those days, on how many days did it rain?	$\frac{2}{3} = \frac{\square}{6}$	Write the number five million, sixteen thousand, four hundred twenty-three.

Name ____________________

Game 80

There are 5,280 feet in 1 mile. How many feet are in 5 miles?	A gallon of paint costs $23.95. Is $200.00 enough to buy 10 gallons?	A car's gas tank holds 16 gallons. The car can go 26 miles on 1 gallon. How many miles can the car go after it is filled with gas?
What numbers come next? 1, 4, 9, 16, 25, ___, ___	$\frac{3}{12} = \frac{\square}{4}$ $\frac{12}{16} = \frac{\square}{4}$	List these numbers from least to greatest. 1.2 5 3.91
I am thinking of an odd number. The sum of the digits is 9. If you round my number to the nearest 10, you get 30. What is my number?	What is $\frac{1}{8}$ of 32?	Lila worked 32.5 hours in April and 27.5 hours in May. How many hours did she work during the 2 months?

Answer Key

Game 1

11 5	7 because it is odd or 8 because it has no straight lines	8 3
28	8 9	52
$18.64	$3.00	9 9

Game 3

14 8	7 because it is not a multiple of 3 or 12 because it is a 2-digit number	3
100	72 feet	60
60	$36.00	6 6

Game 2

13 8	35, 42	49
$0.77	7 + 7 + 5	7,030
15 15	Sunday	Circle the 5.

Game 4

15 7	8	1,010
13	15, 18	15
211	3	30 30

Game 5

14 7	9 because it is not a multiple of 5	4 x 4 = 16
31	32	92
16 8	$5.00	40

Game 7

14 9 5	9	13
154	54, 65	Hana 10 Tim 4
48	36	5 + 4 + 3 = 12

Game 6

16 9 7	7 days	188
61 cents	20 feet	13
348	36	21

Game 8

17 9 8	42	187
seventeen	20	5,112
9	4	39

Game 9

13 9 4	three hundred forty-eight	1,887
24	60	60
10, 8	94 cents	21

Game 11

8	seven thousand twenty-six	5
$3.00	16	Circle the 4, and underline the 6.
6	50	9

Game 10

999; 1,001	46 centimeters	23 13
$1.75	45	65 cents
the answer to an addition problem	8 cents	116

Game 12

15 9 6	6	8
6	9	28
10	75 cents	3,649

Game 13

12 7 5	3	132
September April June November	10 5 4	365
2 2 2	189	12

Game 15

11 3 3	5 3	109 21
351	11:30 A.M.	12 48
21 21	20	1,172

Game 14

Circle the 4, and underline the 6.	3:00 P.M.	5 + 8 + 2 + 2
2 14	1 5	2 6
2,859	24 feet	1,119

Game 16

32 24 8	80 cents	79
26	Monday	$13.94
15 cents	9, 5	16

Game 17

147	60	23
53	52	33, 36
13	93	5

Game 19

$7.32	1,000	$7.32
0 3	$0.84	1,650
919	34	2, 4, 6, 8

Game 18

6 6	2	8 9
$2.22	2 cars 2 bikes or 1 car 3 bikes or 0 cars 5 bikes	90 cents
5	2 hours 15 minutes	18 18

Game 20

18 9	$1.95	19
34	55	1,665
300 1,200	May 23	Possible answers: 45 minutes, 12 hours and 45 minutes, 24 hours and 45 minutes, and so on.

Game 21

16 8	24	$8.50
287	9 6	$22.82
$33.91	24, 30	163

Game 22

12 6	two dollars and fifty cents	832
twenty-one	15; 6	60,809
The twelfth shape is a dark rectangle.	32, 40	two pencils one eraser one ruler

Game 23

$12.15	24 24	
Underline the 1 and circle the 2.	2 hours and 30 minutes	26 points
4 pennies 2 nickels 2 dimes 1 quarter	nine thousand, eight hundred four	983

Game 24

$4.70	28	J
28	13	11 points
	thirty-seven	30

Game 25

14 7	2	12 12
5 8 6 9	25	21
7	36, 45	7

Game 27

96	6 because it is not odd	28 28
October	80 feet	34
2,126	2 nickels and 3 pennies	3,397

Game 26

15 8 7	forty	twenty-six
hundred	24 24	10,201
three	five	eight dollars

Game 28

4	18	6
110	30 30	16
4,135	96	31

Game 29

5	20	48 48
16	3	19 7 78
$9.75	915	$5.79

Game 31

32 32	2:00 p.m.	4 8
Circle the 5 and underline the 0.	4 x 3 x 1 or 4 x 3 ÷ 1	48
12	$1.48	6,538

Game 30

2, 4, 6, 8, 10	7 because it is not a multiple of 3, or 12 because it is even	30
$0.46	$a = 9$ $b = 6$	7:30 P.M.
10	$6.47	35

Game 32

35 35	40	7 5
answer to a division problem	2 and 6 3 and 4 1 and 12	21 7 98 2
3	6	$22.25

Game 33

63 63	643	63 63
301	12:30 P.M.	8 remainder 1
12	$23.84	39

Game 35

28 28	72	32 32
Circle the 5 and underline the 7.	actual width: 2 inches	20
60	actual width: $7\frac{1}{8}$ inches	$3.22

Game 34

54 54	one hundred four hundred	nine six
thirty-six	fourteen	41
eight	eight	12 inches 3 feet 36 inches

Game 36

72 72	52	8 9
May 11, May 18, and May 25	4	Wednesday
22	2,750	36

Game 37

36 36	$45.00	4 9
$125.00	7 8 9 10 sum = 55	60,302
133 remainder 2	Circle the 4, and underline the 7.	12 9 15

Game 39

5	$\frac{9}{10}$	320
4.5	8.4	1,000
144	six and four tenths	215

Game 38

96 inches, or 8 feet	0.1	12 inches, or 1 foot
$17.39	$77.00	2,769
9	22,496	$16.90

Game 40

122	June 30	25
21	15	$69.95
2	7:30 P.M.	20

Game 41

the sum of the lengths of the sides of a polygon	14 centimeters	32 inches
thousand	$64.00	2 x 5 = 10
10 because it is not a multiple of 4 or 8 because it has no straight lines	249	87 remainder 6

Game 43

7 + 8 = 15 8 + 7 = 15 15 – 8 = 7 15 – 7 = 8	34	35
Add 3 each time.	Saturday, October 2	Circle 9,816,290.
6 and 9	51	123 132 213 231 312 321

Game 42

72 17	$1.64	324
4 inches	60	5 feet
8.4 centimeters	9.6	41

Game 44

8 9	60	24
Add 4.	$55.00	470 500
7 and 16	24 26 42 46 62 64	6,151

Game 45

3	54 81	1,849
25 75	Friday, September 3	Circle 4,827,301.
16	89 degrees Fahrenheit	71

Game 47

8 6	4 because it is even	30 miles
a closed plane figure made up of segments called its sides	130	19
3 weeks	Circle 1,230,456.	3 4 4 4 5

Game 46

6 + 7 = 13 7 + 6 = 13 13 – 7 = 6 13 – 6 = 7	4:29	1,000 7,000
2,000	possible answers: 5, 6, 7, or 9	9,002
twenty	3,660	50

Game 48

14 16 2	$11.11	six pieces
thirty-six	Subtract 7.	four quarts eight quarts forty quarts
12, 18, 24, 30	26	4,200

Game 49

5 + 7 = 12 7 + 5 = 12 12 – 5 = 7 12 – 7 = 5	August 31	216
the measure of the inside region 24 square feet	2 dimes 3 nickels 1 penny	16 ounces 80 ounces
41	35, 42, 49, 56, 63, 70	1,889

Game 50

7 7 8 8	252 378	35, 28, 21, 14
63 189	10 and 2	1,788
400	Circle 3,149,567.	18,515

Game 51

9 + 8 = 17 8 + 9 = 17 17 – 8 = 9 17 – 9 = 8	nineteen	204
10	7	1,042
31	5	405

Game 52

9 + 6 = 15 6 + 9 = 15 15 – 6 = 9 15 – 9 = 6	15	72 inches
627	4 weeks	380
1 cow 3 chickens or 2 cows 1 chicken	$103.00	$7.50

Game 53

32 square feet 24 feet	41	13 because it is the only prime number
Circle the 6 and underline the 1.	0	12,400 12,370 12,000
40, 32, 24, 16, 8	1,800	$4.48

Game 55

Circle the 9 and the other 9.	308	40 48
435	1 quarter 1 dime 1 nickel 3 pennies	3
21	16,340	4 + 9 = 13 9 + 4 = 13 13 – 4 = 9 13 – 9 = 4

Game 54

Circle the 17 and 18.	20	Circle the 13 and the 20.
$2.88	14	54,210
34	1,567	$1.80

Game 56

25 square meters 20 meters	17 degrees Fahrenheit	13, 21, 34, 55, 89
152	Wednesday, July 5	38
$1.52 $2.28	64 degrees Fahrenheit	20 and 1

Game 57

12 4 32 2	6 7 9 7	15 45
2,016 square centimeters 200 centimeters	9	$1.91
three tenths	0.05	5 + 7 = 12 7 + 5 = 12 12 – 7 = 5 12 – 5 = 7

Game 58

7 7 5 5	$260.00	56,000
$8.89	80 kilometers	5 kilometers
832 x 9 7,488	2,090 2,100	16

Game 59

72 56 512 8	32 40 20 100	3ft 11in.
two million, thirty-five thousand, one hundred four	7	123 – 54 69
two inches	3,213	three dollars and seventy-five cents

Game 60

7 and 4	$0.92 $1.46	8 and 4
52 feet 144 square feet	million	1,055
8 and 2	Underline the 7 and circle the 8.	4,810 4,800 5,000

Game 61

$5.00	7	12 6 27 3
27	30	608
10	twenty-four and thirty-two hundredths	8

Game 63

63	$3.38	5 3
15	$4.80	84 inches 12 feet
5	13 years old	2

Game 62

Circle 12 + 6.	$2.77	Circle 99 – 98.
$5.59	eighteen	213 26,878
9 90 900	$25.00	12 + 12 + 12

Game 64

39	27	$1.98
36 5	14	one thousand, sixty-eight
1 + 2 + 3 + 4 + 5 + 6 + 7	133	4 shapes (the top 2 and the bottom 2)

Game 65

10 points	289	143
32, 34, 36, 38, 40	128	31, 33, 35, 37, 39
ninth day	$5.30	1,962

Game 67

6	32	1 year = 12 months
1 3	6 and 6	8 1
9 6	4,200,013	5 pennies 4 nickels 0 dimes

Game 66

125	$1.32	119
12 and 7	5 years old	seventy
1,702	$172.00	134

Game 68

1595	1995	22 years
Answer will vary depending on the year.	112	19 years old
1616	80	21

Game 69

12 6 27 3	44.40	432
Multiply by 8.	60	45 5
$6.48	Circle 3, and underline 2.	36 396

Game 71

Circle 3 dozen.	8 9	Circle 13 – 8.
Circle 12, 10, and 1 or circle 12, 8, 3.	32, 64, 128, 256, 512	Circle 5, 2, and 3 or 10, 1, and 3.
day, week, month, year	4 4	quart

Game 70

15 3 54	the chance that something will happen	1 out of 2, or 5 out of 10
306	1	2,678
4 2 5 1	56,000 56,480	4,000

Game 72

teacher observation	8 1 5 6	205
two	7, 14, 21, 28, 35, 42, 49, 56	46
150 158 144 16	32	fifty-one dollars and twenty-two cents

Game 73

teacher observation 0.3	1 or $1\frac{1}{2}$	103,680
18.35	Wednesday	Multiply by 7.
Circle the 9 and underline the 1. 9 ÷ 1 = 9	0.171	9, 18, 27, 36, 45, 54, 63, 72

Game 74

five and forty-three hundredths	1	7.5
$\frac{1}{2}$	4 ways: 2 quarters, 1 dime, 1 nickel 1 quarter, 3 dimes, 2 nickels 1 quarter, 2 dimes, 4 nickels 1 quarter, 1 dime, 6 nickels	20 meters 22.75 square meters
16	3,600 86,400	1.3

Game 75

teacher observation	8.4 meters	8 4
1 6 5 8	6	math
The number is multiplied by itself.	1 x 24 = 24 2 x 12 = 24 3 x 8 = 24 4 x 6 = 24	1, 2, 3, 4, 6, 8, 12, 24

Game 76

a number that divides into another with no remainder	one thousand two hundred one and forty-five hundredths	\$2.15 \$6.45
2.2	8, 16, 24, 32, 40, 48, 56	\$1.18
12 and 3	multiple	Divide by 5.

Game 77

$0.39	5 7 0 2	1,860
6	21	18 6 72 2
594, 549, 954, 945, 459, 495	15	Divide by 2 or cut the first number in half.

Game 78

372	Yes, because 18 inches equals 1 foot 6 inches.	1 out of 6
10	$0.25	$0.25
$12.90 $7.10	0; they are the same.	Yes No

Game 79

four and six hundredths	Circle 52.9 and 21.6.	6.02
Six of the squares should be shaded.	ten people	eight
twelve	4	5,016,423

Game 80

26,400 feet	No	416 miles
36, 49	1 3	1.2, 3.91, 5
27	4	60 hours